Hold Fast

Hebrews 6:4-6 And the Possibility Of Apostasy

Robert E. Picirilli

Hold Fast
Hebrews 6:4-6
And the Possibility of Apostasy

©2023
Robert E. Picirilli
ISBN: 978-0-9966890-7-6
Softcover
All Rights Reserved

No part of this book may be reproduced or transmitted. in any form or by any means, electronic, including photocopying, recording, or any information storage system without permission in writing from the copyright owner.

Scripture References:
King James Bible for Today (KJBT)
King James Version (KJV)
New American Standard Bible (NASB)

Hopeway Publishing
Gate City Virginia 24251
hopewaybooks.com

My Tribute to Robert E. Picirilli

I was converted and called to preach the Gospel in 1964. The Lord led me to attend Free Will Baptist Bible College (now Welch College) in Nashville, Tennessee. So, I left the mountains of Appalachia and followed His leadership.

Having only been saved a couple of years, I did not have a great deal of Bible knowledge. Moving from a very rural mountain area to a large city was quite an adjustment.

There, as a student, I found men of God who loved and taught the Word of God. They loved their students and desired to impart their love for the Word of God to us.

Emphases were always the accuracy and authority of the Word of God. Accurate interpretation and correct application of the Word were also stressed.

Looking back, Dr. Picirilli's impact on my ministry of the Word has been a tremendous blessing. His insistence on the importance of knowing exactly what the writer was saying in the Scriptural context left a lifelong impression on me.

Dr. Picirilli epitomized the best definition of preaching or teaching found in the Bible:
> 4 And Ezra the scribe stood upon a pulpit of wood, which they had built for the purpose . . .
> 8 *So they read in the book of the law of God distinctly, and gave the sense, and caused them to understand the reading.* (Nehemiah 8:4a & 8).

Thank you, Dr. Picirilli
Jim Cox

Preface

I welcome Brother Jim Cox's plan to republish the article in this booklet. I prepared it long ago, and it was published in the fall of 1985 in an issue of *Dimension: A Journal of The Word and Ministry*, sponsored by the Free Will Baptist Bible College Graduate School at that time. Brother Cox seems to think the article may still be helpful. I hope that is the case.

My purpose in writing this article was to provide a thorough exegesis of Hebrews 6:4-6, in its context. This is an important passage for our doctrine that warns against apostasy. That warning is important still. Recent years have seen many professing Christians doing what has come to be called "deconstructing" their faith. In other words, they have turned away from God and the Christian faith, thus demonstrating how real is the danger of apostasy.

I still think it needful, therefore, that we thoroughly analyze the biblical passages that provide these warnings, of which Hebrews 6:4-6 is a prime example. We must ground our beliefs in sound biblical teaching, and to do that, we have to know *exactly* what a passage says. No translation can tell the whole story of the grammar and syntax of the Greek (or Hebrew) original; detailed exegesis is required to fathom the depths and know, precisely, what the text is saying.

I can only hope that this article provides the reader with that kind of understanding. If this occurs, then may our Lord be praised for giving the insight and the truth. Anyone who desires further reading along these lines may find my book helpful:

Grace, Faith, Free Will: Contrasting Views of Salvation: Calvinism & Arminianism (Randall House, 2002).

Hebrews 6:4-6

4 For it is impossible for those who were once enlightened, and have tasted of the heavenly gift, and were made partakers of the Holy Spirit,

5 And have tasted the good word of God, and the powers of the world to come,

6 If they shall fall away, to renew them again unto repentance; seeing they crucify to themselves the Son of God afresh, and put him to an open shame. (KJBT)

Hold Fast

Hebrews 6:4-6
And The Possibility of Apostasy

Robert E. Picirilli

For those of us who believe in the possibility of personal apostasy, Hebrews 6:4-6 is obviously one of the most important passages. It ranks right along with Hebrews 10:26-29 and 2 Peter 2:20-22(see notes)—not to mention several other significant passages—as providing the basis for our teaching on the subject.

The purpose of this article is to present a thorough exegesis of this passage and to treat questions about how it relates to the possibility that a truly regenerate person may "fall from grace." One thing all Christians ought to be able to agree on—whether on this doctrine or not—is that all our teaching should be based on what the Bible has to say and not on traditional philosophical-theological arguments. My aim, then, is to determine exactly what Hebrews 6:4-6 teaches.

THE CONTEXT FOR THE PASSAGE

One of the requirements of good exegesis is to understand how a given passage fits into its context. In this case we should consider the general thrust of Hebrews as a whole. These three verses come in the midst of a book that has perseverance for one of its major themes.

There is no need, here, to review the discussion about the original writer of Hebrews. The inspired text, itself, does not identify its writer.

Nor are we required to establish, for sure, the identity of its original target audience. The inspired text does not tell us that either, the title "To the Hebrews" being a later addition. Even so, the tradition that the "epistle" was first written for Jewish Christians owes its strength to the obvious fact that all its teaching is presented against the backdrop of Jewish ritual. Kent is correct in saying, "Most conservatives would agree that the Hebrew-Christian character of Hebrews is self-evident."[1] He explains the usual understanding of the first readers' situation at the time:

> A careful study of the five warning passages shows their problem to have been the very serious one of wavering before the temptation to leave the Christian movement and retire to the safer haven of Judaism. By such a move, they could avoid persecution from their Jewish kinsmen, and also enjoy the legal protection which Judaism had from the government—a boon which Christians at this time [in the sixties] did not possess.[2]

Even if that should be successfully challenged, the interpretation of our passage would not be significantly affected. Whoever the original readers were, an inductive study of Hebrews by itself makes clear that the readers were considering defection and in need of exhortation to persevere in the faith.

A Theme of Hebrews

One indication of the dominant motif in Hebrews is the frequent occurrence of words urging the readers to hold to the faith. Several of these are on the Greek root *echo*. In 2:1, the King James Version says "we ought to give the more earnest heed to the things which we have heard"; the word translated "give heed" is *prosecho*, meaning "hold on to." In 3:6 we are said to make up Christ's house if we "hold fast"—a good translation of *katecho*. This same word is used again in 3:14, "we have become partakers of Christ if we hold fast," and in 10:23 where we are exhorted to "hold fast."

In 4:14 a different and even more forceful word occurs: *krateo*, which means to cling to, seize, grasp. We are urged to "cling to" our profession—to hold on for dear life. Some writers have cited "let us go on" (6:1) as the key phrase of Hebrews; Griffith Thomas even used this as the name for his commentary.[3] Shank has correctly observed that "let us hold fast" is much more frequent and significant, far more deserving of status as the basic theme of Hebrews.[4]

The Structure of Hebrews

More important than this recurring theme phrase is the pattern of the contents of Hebrews. An exhortation to persevere is at the heart of every major section of the book. Almost everyone will agree that Hebrews gives its consuming interest to convincing the reader that Christ and the New Covenant are

(1) infinitely superior to all that went before and (2) final. This Christological center of interest is certainly the doctrinal passion of the book. But the hortatory concern is

perseverance. Indeed, almost the only practical exhortation contained in the whole book (except for brief miscellaneous exhortations in the concluding chapter) is the exhortation to persevere. As Osborne says, "The willful apostasy of some from the faith" is "the particular problem to which the epistle is addressed."[5]

This concern for perseverance, inseparably linked with a warning against apostasy, is therefore the dominant pastoral concern of Hebrews. It makes up the very "warp and woof" of it, the pattern about which all the cloth is woven. Even the teaching about the superiority and finality of revelation and religion in Christ is reinforcement for the repeated pleas to "hold fast to the faith." As Guthrie puts it, "The writer has no intention of writing a purely academic treatise, but aims throughout to emphasize the practical significance of the points he makes."[6] Marshall notes that the warning passages "are not parentheses...but form an integral part of a structure in which dogmatic theology and practical exhortations are intricately bound up together."[7]

Hebrews is not merely an "epistle" in the usual sense of the word. In form, it closes like one but does not begin like one. In content, it is more like a full-length sermon. (Thus, Buchanan's comment that Hebrews "is a homiletical midrash based on Ps 110." But this gives the "sermon" too narrow a scope.)[8] The text and introduction to this sermon appear in 1:1, 2: God has spoken in various ways in the past, but has given his final and perfect word to us in His Son. The conclusion appears in 12:25-29: You must not refuse Him who speaks; if those who refused him when he spoke in the past did not escape, much more we will not escape if we turn away from Him. This conclusion makes clear the point of the whole message which 13:22 calls a "word of exhortation."

The first section of Hebrews (after the introduction in 1:1-5) is generally agreed to be chapters 1 and 2, which Westcott entitles "The Superiority of the Son, the Mediator of the New Revelation, to Angels."[9] At the heart of this is 2:1-4 (Kent's "First Warning Passage"). Verse 1 literally reads this way: "Because of this, it is necessary for us to be holding on all the more exceedingly to the things heard, lest haply we drift away (from them)." Even those who do not believe that personal apostasy is possible agree that the meaning really is, lest we drift/slip away: "The meaning of the word and its personal subject ("we") indicate not that something might drift away from us, but that 'we' might drift away from something."[10] The word was sometimes used for a boat that had slipped its moorings.

The second section is clearly chapters 3 and 4, "Moses, Joshua, Jesus—the Founders of the Old Economy and of the New."[11] At the heart of this is the passage 3:7-4:2 (Kent's "Second Warning Passage," which he extends to 4:13). There we read (literally): "Be on watch, brothers, lest haply there will be in anyone of you a wicked, unbelieving heart in departing from the living God" (3:12). "Departing" is the very Greek root that our English "apostasy" comes from (the verb *apostenai*; the noun is *apostasia*), "an unbelief which abandons hope."[12] The writer is saying, simply: "Brothers, be on guard against apostatizing from God."

As Lenski defines: "Unbelief is thus understood in the sense of once having believed in the living God and then having turned away from him."[13] Bruce compares "the action of the Israelites when they 'turned back in their hearts unto Egypt'...a gesture of outright apostasy, a complete break with God."[14] Guthrie: "the greatest defection possible."[15]

We also read, in this section (literally): "We have come to be partakers of Christ, if in fact we hold fast [the theme word discussed above] the beginning of our confidence firm unto the end" (3:14). Westcott says, "That which has been stated as fact [that is, having become partakers of Christ] is now made conditional in its permanence on the maintenance of faith."[16]

The third and central section is Chapters 5-7: "The High Priesthood of Christ, Universal and Sovereign."[17] At the heart of this is the extended exhortation of 5:11-6:12 (Kent's "Third Warning Passage," 5:11-6:20). Since this is the passage that contains 6:4-6, further comment is saved for the next section of this article.

The final section is chapters 8-12, although many interpreters prefer to make this into two sections, 8:1-10:18 and 10:19-12:29. (If I were going to divide this section into two main parts, I would divide at 11:1; then each of the teaching parts would be concluded with exhortation. But this technicality does not need to be pursued here.) There are two extended passages of exhortation woven into these five chapters.

Kent's "Fourth Warning Passage" is 10:26-31; actually, the exhortation extends from 10:10-39. Once again, we are urged (literally), "Let us be holding fast [the theme word, again] the confession of hope unwavering" (10:23). And to this is attached the terrible warning of vss. 26-31: if we will to take back up our sinful ways, thus trampling under foot

Christ's blood and doing insult to the Spirit, our punishment will be much worse than death without mercy as prescribed in the Mosaic economy. Citing the favorite text for justification by faith, "The just shall live by faith," the writer adds (from the same source in the Greek Old Testament), "but if he (the just one) draws back, my soul has no pleasure in him" (v. 38).

Westcott observes, correctly, that it is altogether unwarranted to read the inserted "any man" of the King James Version as though this is someone other than "the just one."[18] The inspired reader of Hebrews is referring, specifically, to the "drawing back" of one justified by faith, leading to this pronouncement by God.

The final extensive exhortation serves as the conclusion to the "sermon" and includes all of chapter 12 (although Kent includes, in his "Fifth Warning Passage," only 12:18-29). Here we are warned "lest anyone fall back from (Westcott: "implying a moral separation" from)[19] the grace of God" (v. 15). The writer backs this up with the example of Esau as one for whom no place of repentance and restoration to what he had lost could be found. The serious conclusion, then, is that we will not escape if we "turn back from" the One (who is and speaks to us) from heaven. Actually, the writer does not present this in a merely hypothetical manner; literally, the words are "we who are turning back from." He evidently regards the process of apostasy as having already begun and identifies himself with his people in this awful thing.

It is clear, then, that 6:4-6 is at the heart of a book that has the question of apostasy and perseverance at its very roots. The five warning passages tie the "sermon" together and reveal that its main thrust is to exhort the audience to hold fast to the faith they have placed in Christ lest apostasy occur, lest they forsake the very One God has revealed as providing, by His redemptive work, room for them to stand righteous before God. There is no sacrifice for sins, no provision for righteousness, outside Him. Such is the context of 6:4-6.

(I would observe, in passing, that a good principle of Biblical interpretation is to get one's basic doctrine about a subject from a place where that subject is clearly being discussed, rather than from a passing mention. Thus, any doctrine of perseverance ought to involve Hebrews as a primary source.)

THE TEXT

To begin with, here is my own more or less literal translation of the passage (from the Greek), arranged so that the reader can more clearly see the relationship of the clauses:

> For it is impossible for
>> those who were once-for-all enlightened
>> and who tasted of the heavenly free gift
>> and who became partakers of the Holy Spirit
>> and who tasted God's good word and the powers of the coming age
>> and who fell away
>
> to be being renewed again unto repentance,
> they crucifying again to/for themselves the Son of God and exposing (Him) to public shame.

The exegesis and interpretation of these words involve three key questions about the experience of the persons the writer is describing. (For the moment, this need not involve discussion whether he means people that had actually experienced all this or simply people who were candidates for it.)

Does this describe the real experience of salvation?

This question arises because some interpreters suggest that something less than genuine conversion is meant. The people referred to are said to have experienced four positive things, so that the question whether they were truly regenerate depends on the meaning of those four clauses, as follows.

(1) *They were once-for-all enlightened.* This appears, by any way of reading it, to refer to the spiritual enlightenment of those truly saved. The Greek verb (*photizomai*) means to give one light or bring him into light. The very same description is used again in 10:32, where also there is no reason to doubt that it is deliberately meant, by itself, as a synonym for conversion. The Biblical background involved is the contrast between darkness and light and between those in the darkness and those in the light (cf. 2 Cor. 4:4).

The word translated "once" (Greek *hapax*) has the idea of "once for all" or "once effectively." This same word occurs several times in Hebrews, and comparing them is instructive: 9:7, 26, 27, 28; 10:2; 12:26, 27. In these other places the word consciously implies something done once in a way that no repetition or addition is needed to complete it. Kent acknowledges that "the use of 'once for all' points to something complete, rather than partial or inadequate."[20]

(2) *They tasted of the heavenly free gift.* Two points have sometimes been made against equating this with genuine salvation. One is the use of "tasting," said by some to imply a partial rather than a full experience. But that objection reflects a modem English idiom rather than the way the ancient Greeks used this verb (*geuomai*). Even when referring to food, they could use this word for full-fledged eating, as in Acts 10:10. More important, they used this word metaphorically to mean "experience." Especially significant is the fact that the writer of Hebrews used this very same verb in 2:9 to refer to Christ's "experiencing" death. Surely no one would wish to say that He only partially or incompletely experienced death.

The other objection is more technical: namely, that "taste" is followed, here, by the genitive object rather than by the accusative object (in Greek). The genitive case merely identifies, indicating which one or what kind, while the accusative is the case of extent. The objectors say this means only that the people described tasted of the gift, but did not taste the gift to its full extent. Two things are wrong with this objection. First, while the genitive does not expressly speak of extent, neither does it deny it; the Greek writer would not have to use it even when extent was true. Second, and more important, the genitive object is also used in 2:9! (Further, see below on the fourth clause.)

The people being described, then, "experienced" the heavenly free gift. Interpreters do not all agree on exactly what this "heavenly free gift" is, but the disagreement does not affect the issue at hand and the general meaning is clear. Probably the best answer is that it means salvation and what goes with it: justification and eternal life in Christ: "salvation blessings."[21] The various interpreters suggest salvation, eternal life, forgiveness of sins, the Holy Spirit, or Christ Himself.

(3) *They became partakers of the Holy Spirit.* Guthrie observes, "The idea of sharing the Holy Spirit is remarkable. This at once distinguishes the person from one who has no more than a nodding acquaintance with Christianity."[22] The word "partakers" (Greek *metochoi*), which means "to have together with," is apparently used by the writer of Hebrews exclusively to refer to Christians' common participation in things related to their salvation. In 3:1 we are "partakers" of the heavenly calling; in 3:14 "partakers" of Christ; and in 12:8 "partakers" of the discipline that distinguishes true sons from bastards. Either of these three or the one here, would by itself be adequate to identify such a "partaker" as a Christian.

To have the Holy Spirit, in common with other believers, is certainly to be a Christian. Receiving the gift of the Spirit, in the New Testament, is a regular way of stating what it means to become a Christian. (See Acts 2:38, 39 and Gal. 3:14 for just two of many examples.)

(4) *They tasted God's good word and the powers of the coming age*. We meet "tasting" again; see above on the second clause. If any doubt should remain, about the fact that the genitive object was used in the clause above, this one will remove that doubt. The accusative object is used here.

Those described have "experienced" God's good word. This means that they have experienced the goodness that God has spoken of. God has spoken good to those who put faith in Him, and these have put what God has said to the test and experienced that good. As Kent puts it, this is "experiencing the word of God in the gospel and finding it good."[23] (Compare 1 Pet. 2:3.)

Furthermore, they have "experienced" the powers of the coming age. The word translated "powers" (Greek *dunameis*) often means "miracles" (as in 2:4). In its broadest sense, that is the idea here: supernatural workings. Manifestations of Divine power do not have their origin in this present age. All the mighty works of God are from the age to come, "other-world powers" as Lenski puts it.[24] But Christians, still living in this present age, have already begun to experience the supernatural workings characteristic of the age to come. This includes more than we need to discuss here ("spiritual gifts," for example), but regeneration and the gift of the Spirit are the initial powerful works of the age to come that all Christians have in common.

Osborne points out that "the age to come" is important in the eschatology of Hebrews, where "Eschatology becomes a part of soteriology"; thus, this phrase implies a foretaste of "kingdom blessings."[25] J. Behm, discussing all the "taste" clauses in this verse, says that they describe "vividly the reality of personal experiences of salvation enjoyed by Christians at conversion."[26]

In reference to these four clauses as a whole, then, we may say that one would be hard put to find a better description of genuine conversion. Either of the clauses will stand by itself in this respect; all four of them together provide one of the finest statements about salvation, from its experiential side, that appears anywhere in Scripture.

Does this describe apostasy from salvation?

The answer to this question resides in the meaning of the clause which the King James Version renders, "If they shall fall away."

There is not much dispute about the meaning of the words. In light of the impossibility of repentance mentioned (to be discussed below), most interpreters readily accept the fact that to "fall away" (Greek *parapipto*) leaves a person outside a saving relationship to Christ. (This is the only time this verb occurs in the New Testament; it occurs in the Greek translation of the Old Testament in passages that also refer to apostasy: Ezek. 18:24, for example.) As Kent (who does not believe apostasy is possible) expresses it, the words mean "complete and final repudiation of Christ (as in 10:26, 27)...[describing]...those who are regenerated and then repudiate Christ and forsake Hirn."[27] The "falling away" is defection from the experience described in the four positive clauses that precede.

That is what apostasy means. In light of the contents of the entire book of Hebrews, as outlined above, the "falling away" is evidently synonymous with "drifting away" (2:1), with "departing from [precisely, apostatizing from] the living God" (3:12), with "drawing back" (10:38), with "turning away from the One from heaven" (12:25).

Some interpreters, perhaps unfamiliar with the Greek original, misunderstand the relationship of the clauses. They readily acknowledge that the first four positive clauses describe a truly regenerate state. Then they add (using the King James Version wording) that such regenerate persons as these, if they should fall away, could not possibly be renewed to repentance. Note the emphasis on the "if." In fact, they say, this is a purely hypothetical addition: the truly regenerate cannot fall away.

But the grammar of the original will not allow this construction. The fifth clause cannot be made a merely hypothetical attachment to an otherwise real set of circumstances. The literal translation I gave at the beginning of this section shows this in English. In Greek the grammar is equally clear. What we have are five equal, coordinate, aorist-tense (simple past action in this context) participles in a series. (The King James Version translators introduced the "if," I assume, to make the long sentence smoother and more readable.) The persons that the writer of Hebrews uses for his lesson have done all five things equally: they are persons who were enlightened, and tasted the heavenly gift, and became partakers of the Spirit, and tasted God's good word and the powers of the world to come, and fell away. That is exactly the way the Greek reads. Kent recognizes this: "Grammatically there is no warrant for treating the last [participle] in the series any differently from the others."[28] The New American Standard Bible gives an especially clear and accurate translation: "In the case of those who have once been enlightened ...and then have fallen away, it is impossible to renew them again to repentance."

(It would be possible to avoid this grammatical hurdle by making the entire illustration, rather than just the last of the five coordinate clauses, hypothetical. This will be discussed below.)

What is the nature of the impossibility referred to?

Of those who have experienced the five things listed, the writer says that it is not possible to be renewing them again unto repentance. The affirmation of this is quite strong: for emphasis the word impossible is moved up to be the very first word in the whole sentence. Two things are involved, although they cannot be separated.

First, one must consider what is impossible: for those who are converted and fall away, renewal unto repentance. The "renewal" makes clear that there had been repentance earlier. Repentance is a complete change of mind and attitude. Now that the falling away has taken place, repentance from that apostate state is not possible. All this seems obvious from the words themselves.

Repentance has already been introduced into the immediate context. In vss. 1-3 the writer has said that we ought, in our experience, to let ourselves be carried along toward maturity rather than putting down again (among other things) the foundation of "repentance from dead works." For (he adds in vss. 4-6) the person who is converted and falls away cannot be renewed unto repentance. Clearly, then, the same repentance is meant, the repentance from dead works that comes at conversion.

The association of "repentance" with a warning against apostasy in 12:15-17 strengthens this understanding. The warning "lest anyone fall back from the grace of God" is linked to the case of Esau for whom "a place (opportunity) of repentance was not found"—one that would enable him to receive the inheritance that was originally his.

The second consideration is why there is no possibility for repentance. The explanation is contained in the words of the King James Version, "seeing they crucify to themselves the Son of God afresh, and put him to an open shame." The translators supplied "seeing"; the literal words (participles again) are, "re-crucifying to (or for) themselves the Son of God and exposing (Him) to public shame." The cross, in Roman times, was an object of special shame. Apostates are here "identified with those whose hatred of Christ led them to exhibit him as an object of contempt on a hated Roman gibbet."[29]

A very few interpreters would argue that this is not a reason at all, and that the King James translators therefore made a poor choice of words when they used "seeing." The technicalities of the grammar are that these participles are circumstantial, which leaves the interpreter to determine from the context just what kind of circumstances are meant. Thus, Shank offers his opinion that these are circumstances of time and not of cause (as in the King James Version). He would translate, then, this way: "It is impossible to renew them again to repentance so long as they are crucifying...and publicly shaming Him."[30]

Such a view leads to the conclusion that the apostasy described here can be remedied, that repentance from apostasy back to God is not finally impossible after all, that the writer only means a temporary impossibility. Westcott (even though he, unlike Shank, regards the circumstantial participle as causal) believes that the passage teaches apostasy, and that the apostasy can be remedied: "The moral cause of the impossibility which has been affirmed....is an active, continuous hostility to Christ in the souls of such men.[31] He therefore limits the impossibility to human agency and suggests that divine agency can accomplish, in such a case, a restoration from death to life (technically, not another new birth).[32] I agree with Marshall, that "The passage gives us no right to assert that there may be a special intervention of God to restore those whom men cannot restore."[33]

Very few interpreters will accept that the apostasy described here can be remedied. There are several good arguments against it. For one thing, the clause simply does not fit as a temporal clause; it "feels right" only as causal, and the interpreters and translators are nearly unanimous in rendering it: "It is impossible...because ("seeing") they are re-crucifying Him."

For another thing, the emphasis on the impossible, as noted above, makes more sense if it is a final impossibility. Shank's interpretation winds up saying that it is impossible to renew them to repentance so long as they persist in their attitude of rejection—which is not much of a point, since it is always impossible to bring anyone to repentance as long as he persists in rejection: "a truism hardly worth putting into words."[34] This almost amounts to saying that it is impossible to bring him to repentance so long as he persists in an attitude that makes it impossible to bring him to repentance, and that is pure tautology. Westcott's way of putting it is not quite that weak. What he is saying is that it is impossible for men to bring this person back to repentance because of his ongoing, active hostility to Christ. But that does not seem to do justice to the sentence either; it is always impossible for men to produce repentance without Divine agency.

For another thing, one must do justice to the point of vv. 7, 8. The "for" in v. 7 attaches these two verses to vv. 4-6 as a reason, given in the form of an illustration. Thus, the impossibility of vv. 4-6 lies not merely in the attitude of the apostate but also in the judgment of God. The land in the illustration is "reprobate land"[35]—Greek *adokimos* (as in 1 Cor. 9:27, "castaway").

Finally, one more reason for regarding the apostasy of w. 4-6 as final is found in the other passages about apostasy in Hebrews, as listed earlier in this article. Thus 2:1-4 asks how we shall escape if we "drift away" from this great salvation, implying that there is no escape. The passage beginning at 3:7 backs up its warning against apostasy by reminding us of the Israelites to whom God swore that they would not enter the promised rest. In 12:25, again, the warning is that we will not escape if we turn away from Him.

Especially does 10:26-39 shed light on the serious finality of apostasy. This passage warns that God will take no pleasure in the one who draws back (v. 38); Bruce speaks of this as "the divine displeasure which will rest upon him."[36] The passage also provides us with the true reason for the impossibility: for the one who wills to return to sin, thus treading under foot the blood of Christ's sacrifice for sin and insulting the Spirit of grace, there "remaineth no more sacrifice for sins." Christ's blood is the only atonement for sin; having experienced and then rejected that, there is nowhere else the apostate can turn. The re-crucifying and public exposure of Christ in 6:6 seems clearly to refer to the same thing as treading under foot the Son of God and counting His atoning blood an unholy thing in 10:29.

For all these reasons, then, it seems clear that the apostasy of these verses is final apostasy (not simply what some call "backsliding") and that this apostasy cannot be remedied.

OTHER READINGS OF THE TEXT

Briefly, and in summary fashion, notice should be taken of the views of those who disagree with the position taken above. Among those who do not believe that personal apostasy from faith in Christ is possible, there are two main ways of explaining the meaning of Hebrews 6:4-6.

The first is to say that the people described here are not meant to be pictured as truly regenerate. As Kenneth Wuest puts it, the "apostasy" referred to in Hebrews is "the act of an unsaved Jew...renouncing his professed faith in Messiah."[37] Among those who hold this view are Bruce and Morris. Bruce compares these to people "immunized against a disease by being inoculated with a mild form of it...something which, for the time being, looks so like the real thing that it is genuinely mistaken for it."[38] Morris compares Simon Magus, quoting Acts 8:13, that he "believed and was baptized. And he followed Philip everywhere." He observes: "This is as definite as anything in Hebrews 6."[39] In fact, everything in Hebrews 6:4, 5 is more definite than that.

This approach has already been answered above and need not be discussed at length again. The fact is that the four positive participles describe, in the clearest way possible, genuine conversion. Even Kent hits the nail on the head when he says that he "doubts whether the same description if found elsewhere would ever be explained by these interpreters in any way other than full regeneration."[40]

The other approach is to say that the writer is dealing only with a hypothetical situation. I have noted, above, that it simply will not do to treat the four positive participles as real and then treat the fifth as hypothetical. But some interpreters treat the entire description as hypothetical. In other words, they say that the passage really describes one who is truly regenerate and then commits apostasy. However, they say, such a case is hypothetical and cannot really occur.

Such is Kent's view. He suggests that "The author has described a supposed case, assuming for the moment the presuppositions of some of his confused and wavering readers."[41] In other words, assuming that the readers, true Christians, were being tempted to forsake Christianity and return to Judaism, the writer is showing them the folly of their consideration by saying that a person who was truly saved and forsook Christ could never again be saved. "The believers (seeing what an awful consequence apostasy would have, if it were possible), would be warned by this statement to remain firm (and from the human standpoint the warnings of Scripture are a means to ensure the perseverance of the saints)."[42]

Kent quotes Westcott for this explanation: "The case is hypothetical. There is nothing to show that the conditions of fatal apostasy had been fulfilled, still less that they had been fulfilled in the case of any of these addressed. Indeed, the contrary is assumed: vs. 9 ff."[43] But he is clearly mistaken in his reading of Westcott, who means something else entirely by the word "hypothetical." Westcott only means that the writer of Hebrews assumes that his readers had not yet apostatized, not that they could not.

Guthrie understands Westcott more correctly: "The writer appears to be reflecting on a hypothetical case, although in the nature of the whole argument, it must be supposed that it was a real possibility."[44] In that sense, I am inclined to agree that the writer is not necessarily describing people among his readers who had already committed apostasy, as 6:9 implies. At the same time, I am confident that the passage describes actual possibility, even if an extreme case. For the writer to describe what awful consequences would result if people were saved and apostatized carries no warning value at all if it cannot really happen. As Morris puts it, "Unless he is speaking of a real possibility his warning means nothing."[45]

Furthermore, the grammar of the passage is against reading it as a merely hypothetical construction. The Greeks had several ways to present hypothetical propositions: the subjunctive mode, the optative mode, even the imperfect of the indicative mode (as in 11:15, for example). But aorist participles, used as they are in this sentence, simply do not convey hypothesis.

(I have counted 77 other instances of the aorist participle in Hebrews, and not one of them is hypothetical—unless one counts these in 6 and those in 10:29, where the grammatical structure is similar.)

If we look not at the participles but at the main clause, the writer is forthrightly saying that "It is impossible to renew such to repentance"—not that it would be impossible to renew them. The construction is the same as in 6:18 (It is impossible for God to lie), 10:4 (It is impossible for the blood of bulls and goats to take away sin), and 11:6 (It is impossible to please God without faith). In every way, then, the writer is saying, in a straightforward manner, that it is not possible to renew those who did these five things to repentance. This warning, considered by itself or in association with the repeated warnings of the whole book, is so effective because it is so possible. (I suggest that one who did not already have his mind made up that apostasy is not possible would not think the writer's illustration merely hypothetical. Once more, I recommend the NASB translation of these verses.)

Having considered how the text is read by those who do not believe apostasy is possible, we should add, for sake of completeness, that those who believe apostasy is possible but also believe it can be remedied, read the text in a manner different from the view I have set forth. I mentioned, earlier, the (somewhat different) views of Shank and Westcott to this effect. There is no need to repeat, here, the arguments already given. I only add that the other instances of "impossible" in Hebrews (6:18; 10:4; 11:6, as cited in the preceding paragraph) also add weight to the view that the writer is using the word to refer not to a temporary "impossibility" but to something impossible by nature; Guthrie: "The statements are all absolutes."[46]

CONCLUSION

It was not the purpose of this article to present a complete treatment of the subject of apostasy, but to give a thorough exegesis of Hebrews 6:4-6 in its context. This much seems too clear to dispute: that personal apostasy from a truly regenerate condition really is possible, and that there is no recovery from such a final apostasy.

This apostasy is, therefore, something much more serious than what people generally mean by "backsliding." Since salvation is, first and always, by faith, this apostasy involves a willful departure from the saving knowledge of Christ, a final retraction of faith from Him in whom alone is provision for forgiveness of sin. The apostate forsakes the cross where he found forgiveness; as Bruce comments, "By renouncing Christ they put themselves in the position of those who, deliberately refusing His claim to be the Son of God, had Him crucified and exposed to public shame."[47]

I should probably add that such an apostate will not desire to find forgiveness in Christ: that is the very thing he has turned away from. Those who sincerely desire forgiveness and fellowship with God have not committed apostasy.

I should also add that my purpose has not included developing the practical implications of this teaching. As a summary of these implications, the words of Osborne express them well: "The only remedy (against the danger of apostasy) is a constant perseverance in the faith, and a continual growth to Christian maturity."[48] Also, to be noted is that the writer of Hebrews "calls his readers to assist each other by mutual exhortation on their pilgrimage journey"[49] (see 3:13; 10:24f; 12:12f; 13:17).

Notes

Hebrews 10:26-39

26 For if we sin willfully after that we have received the knowledge of the truth, there remains no more sacrifice for sins,
27 But a certain fearful looking forward to judgment and fiery indignation, which shall devour the adversaries.
28 He who despised Moses' law died without mercy under two or three witnesses:
29 Of how much worse punishment, do you suppose, shall he be thought worthy, who has trodden underfoot the Son of God, and has counted the blood of the covenant, with which he was sanctified, an unholy thing, and has insulted the Spirit of grace

30 For we know him who has said, Vengeance belongs unto me, I will repay, says the Lord. And again, The Lord shall judge his people.

31 It is a fearful thing to fall into the hands of the living God.

32 But remember the former days, in which, after you were illuminated, you endured a great struggle with afflictions;

33 Partly, while you were made a gazing stock both by reproaches and afflictions; and partly, while you became companions of those who were so treated.

34 For you had compassion on me in my chains, and took joyfully the spoiling of your goods, knowing in yourselves that you have in heaven a better and an enduring possession.

35 Therefore do not throw away your confidence, which has great compensation of reward.

36 For you need to have patience, that, after you have done the will of God, you might receive the promise.

37 For yet a little while, and he who shall come will come, and will not delay.

38 Now the just shall live by faith: but if any man draws back, my soul shall have no pleasure in him.

39 But we are not of those who draw back unto perdition; but of those who believe to the saving of the soul. (KJBT)

II Peter 2:20-22

20 For if after they have escaped the pollutions of the world through the knowledge of the Lord and Savior Jesus Christ, they are again entangled in it, and overcome, the latter end is worse for them than the beginning.

21 For it had been better for them not to have known the way of righteousness, than, after they have known it, to turn from the holy commandment delivered unto them.

22 But it has happened unto them according to the true proverb, The dog has returned to his own vomit; and the sow that was washed returned to her wallowing in the mud. (KJBT)

Endnotes

[1] Homer A. Kent, *The Epistle to the Hebrews: A Commentary* (BMH Books, 1972), 23.
[2] *Ibid.*, 25.
[3] W. H. Griffith Thomas, *"Let Us Go On"* (Zondervan, 1944).
[4] Robert Shank, *Life in the Son* (Westcott Publishers, l960), 233.
[5] Grant R. Osborne, *"Soteriology in the Epistle to the Hebrews,"* in Grace Unlimited, ed. Clark Pinnock (Bethany, 1975), 146.
[6] Donald Guthrie, *Hebrews* (Tyndale NT Commentaries: Inter-Varsity, 1983), 83.
[7] Howard Marshall, *Kept By the Power of God* (Bethany, 1969), 139.
[8] George Wesley Buchanan, *To The Hebrews* (Anchor Bible: Doubleday, 1972), xix.
[9] B. F. Westcott, *The Epistle to the Hebrews* (Eerdmans, 1955), xlvii.
[10] Kent, 47.
[11] Wescott, xlviii.
[12] *Theological Dictionary of the New Testament* (Eerdmans, 1972; hereafter identified as TDNT), 1:513.
[13] R.C.H. Lenski, *The Interpretation of The Epistle to the Hebrews and The Epistle of James* (Wartburg Press, l956), 118.
[14] F. F. Bruce, *The Epistle to the Hebrews* (New International Commentary of the NT: Eerdmans, 1964), 64.
[15] Guthrie, 106.
[16] Westcott, 85.
[17] *Ibid.,* xlix.
[18] *Ibid.,* 337.
[19] *Ibid.,* 406.
[20] Kent, 108.
[21] Osborne, 149.
[22] Guthrie, 142.
[23] Kent, 109.
[24] Lenski, 184.
[25] Osborne, 148, 149.
[26] *TDNT*, 1:676.
[27] Kent, 110.

[28] *Ibid.*, 108.
[29] Guthrie, 144.
[30] Shank, 318.
[31] Wescott, 151.
[32] *Ibid.*, 150, 165.
[33] Marshall, 142.
[34] Bruce, 124.
[35] *Ibid.*, 125.
[36] *Ibid.*, 274.
[37] Kenneth S. Wuest, "Hebrews Six in the Greek New Testament," *Bibliotheca Sacra* 119 (1962), 46.
[38] Bruce, 118, 119.
[39] Leon Morris, *Hebrews* (Bible Study Commentary: Zondervan, 1983), 59.
[40] Kent, 112.
[41] *Ibid.*, 113.
[42] *Ibid.*
[43] Westcott, 165.
[44] Guthrie, 145.
[45] Morris, 59.
[46] Guthrie, 141.
[47] Bruce, 124.
[48] Osborne, 153.
[49] Marshall, 153.

www.ingramcontent.com/pod-product-compliance
Lightning Source LLC
Chambersburg PA
CBHW070443010526
44118CB00014B/2169